Francisco Carvalho Pereira

Determining characteristics of mayoral elections in Brazil

AF671629

Francisco Carvalho Pereira

Determining characteristics of mayoral elections in Brazil

Data mining as a tool for discovering patterns in municipal election data

ScienciaScripts

Imprint
Any brand names and product names mentioned in this book are subject to trademark, brand or patent protection and are trademarks or registered trademarks of their respective holders. The use of brand names, product names, common names, trade names, product descriptions etc. even without a particular marking in this work is in no way to be construed to mean that such names may be regarded as unrestricted in respect of trademark and brand protection legislation and could thus be used by anyone.

Cover image: www.ingimage.com

This book is a translation from the original published under ISBN 978-3-330-77304-2.

Publisher:
Sciencia Scripts
is a trademark of
Dodo Books Indian Ocean Ltd. and OmniScriptum S.R.L publishing group

120 High Road, East Finchley, London, N2 9ED, United Kingdom
Str. Armeneasca 28/1, office 1, Chisinau MD-2012, Republic of Moldova, Europe
Managing Directors: Ieva Konstantinova, Victoria Ursu
info@omniscriptum.com

Printed at: see last page
ISBN: 978-620-8-64619-6

Copyright © Francisco Carvalho Pereira
Copyright © 2025 Dodo Books Indian Ocean Ltd. and OmniScriptum S.R.L publishing group

SUMMARY

"I'm not obliged to live, but I have a duty to be true. I'm not obliged to be successful, but I have a duty to respond to the Light I have."

Abraham Lineoln

SUMMARY

Brazil's current political situation provides citizens with the broad right to vote, underpinned by a democratic regime characterized by political freedom. This freedom means that there can be multiple parties and candidates, making it necessary for voters to seek out information about the contenders, often in the media or in their own environment. After each election is over, a lot of data is generated which, when totaled up, indicates which candidates have been elected. But this data is not enough to tell us why a candidate was elected, i.e. what factor influenced the choice of their name on the ballot. To find out what these factors are, you need to analyze other types of data, in addition to those generated on election day. This data is made available by the TSE (Superior Electoral Court), where it is possible to find out age, profession, level of education, marital status, among other information about each candidate. With this data in hand, it is possible to relate it to the election data and find out how much each characteristic influences the final result. Data mining is a useful tool for extracting this knowledge, as it deals with large databases, looking for previously unknown patterns. The purpose of this work is to use the J48 data classification algorithm, with the help of the WEKA tool, to carry out this task, being able to classify data relating to the 2012 mayoral elections in the five regions of Brazil, selecting one state from each region. The results showed that factors such as the candidate's political experience, campaign spending and age directly influenced the outcome of the election, as well as other factors such as total assets and level of education.

Keywords: data mining, data classification, pattern discovery.

1 INTRODUCTION

With every election that takes place in Brazil, new Candidates run for public office, seeking to win over the electorate and achieve their dream political career. In addition, voters are becoming more and more critical, due to the increased availability of information about candidates, making voting an even more careful choice.

In addition to the most common sources of electoral publicity, the internet is increasingly being used. According to Figueira (2013), the internet creates non-hierarchical conversational spaces, changing the campaign experience by disseminating political opinions through social media.

Information about the candidates is therefore easy to find, which makes the candidate's political or professional life a major influence on the choice of candidate. In addition to this important factor, others come to the fore, such as the total investment in the political campaign, which often leads to greater spending on advertising, and the characteristics of the candidate, such as age, gender and profession, which can influence the choice of candidate.

The election is described by Oliveira (2012) as a representation of the electoral process, in other words, it is the account of how the voter voted, and in which socio-economic, ideological or religious segments a candidate achieved the most votes. The author also states that deciphering the electoral phenomenon goes beyond this aspect; it means identifying the causes that motivate or lead an individual or group of individuals to make this important decision. By identifying behavior in elections, social phenomena, more precisely electoral phenomena, are elucidated.

Given the amount of data available from each election, it is interesting to assess how much each of the above factors determines the final result. To help with this evaluation, data mining is fundamental, as it can be used to extract this information.

The task of data mining requires defining a scope for the study, i.e. defining which data will be used, for example by choosing a category of candidate, or selecting by federative unit, in order to reduce the amount of data and make it easier to analyze.

The proposal is therefore to use data from mayoral candidates, as this is a position that requires the elected candidate to have a higher proportion of votes than other positions, such as councillor. In addition, the position of mayor has a smaller number of candidates per city, which reduces the amount of data to be analyzed.

In addition to defining the type of candidacy to be studied, it was necessary to further delimit the data, because considering the number of municipalities in the country, it would be impossible to analyze all the data available. Therefore, 5 (five) Brazilian states, Rio Grande do Sul, Sao Paulo, Bahia, Para and Goias, were defined as the target, one from each region of Brazil, thus including all its municipalities. After this definition, the data from the chosen states was mined and the results compared.

Bearing in mind the complexity involved in the data mining process, it is important to use an appropriate tool with algorithms to extract the desired knowledge. The WEKA tool[2] (*Waikato Environment for Knowledge Analysis*), developed by the University of Waikato in New Zealand, was chosen to fulfill this objective.

As mentioned by Witten and Frank (2005), the WEKA tool provides a variety of functions for transforming a data set, including algorithms of various kinds, allowing you to process a data set, based on a learning scheme, and analyze the results and performance, all without having to write any code.

With this tool, knowledge can be extracted from the database under study, and we can find out how much factors such as age, gender, profession and total campaign investment were decisive for the election of candidates.

1.1 General Objective

To find possible patterns in electoral data of mayoral candidates from the 2012 elections in Brazil, indicating possible relevant trends, using data mining techniques available in the WEKA tool.

1.2 Specific Objectives

- Filtering and standardization of available data;
- Processing and capturing results using WEKA;
- Analysis of the results obtained.

1.3 Work structure

This work has 5 more sections:

- Section 2 (Brazil's political situation): provides a brief description of Brazil's political situation, as well as important aspects relating to voters and the factors that influence voting.
- Section 3 (Data mining): presents some authors' concepts on data mining, including the main methods and algorithms.
- Section 4 (Development): this section shows the steps in the development of the work proposal.
- Section 5 (Methodology): this chapter identifies the development topics and how each stage

1 Available at http://www.cs.waikato.ac.nz/ml/weka/

was carried out.

- Section 6 (Conclusion): in this stage the final conclusions are presented, based on the results obtained.

2 BRAZIL'S POLITICAL SITUATION

Brazil is currently experiencing a period of democracy, marked mainly by the broad right of citizens to vote. This scenario began to be built by the popular movement known as *Diretas Jà*, one of the largest in Brazilian history, which arose from the *Dante de OHveira Amendment*, culminating in the constituent assembly that subsequently drew up the 1988 constitution, establishing Brazilian democracy. Earlier, on January 15, 1985, Tancredo Neves was elected president, marking the beginning of the so-called *New Republic* (LIMA, 2012).

According to Felisbino et al. (2012), in 2008 Brazil completed 22 years of civilian rule and 19 years of democratic experience, based on the 1988 Federal Constitution. According to the author, nowadays, with the current political maturity, there is no fear of a return to military rule, because the members of the political elite and the people know that democracy is above any other regime and believe it to be the best option for the country.

2.1 Political leadership and public office

One of the factors that most influences the likelihood of a candidate occupying a political post is the hierarchical social position or social position of origin of the candidate, such as the last profession before occupying the post. Regardless of the position being considered, be it mayor, manager, deputy or councillor, most of these positions are held by members of the upper classes of society, such as large farmers, industrialists and big businessmen, executives and various intellectuals. In this way, parliamentary representation projects an inverted image of the social structure, considering that more than three quarters of MPs come from the most socially and culturally advantaged part of the population (GAXIE, 2012).

Another important factor to note is the number of candidates each city had in the last elections. Rodrigues (2011) cites that in 2004, 14 people ran for mayor in the first round of elections in the city of São Paulo, and in the same year, only one candidate ran in the election in the city of Bom Jardim da Serra (SC), and obviously won.

One of the possible explanations for this, according to Rodrigues (2011), is that the institutional structure determines the number of candidates, so that the presence of direct elections and a single round of voting influences the number of contestants, a justification that is often mentioned for the large number of elections with only two candidates for the presidency of the United States. On the other hand, as the author also mentions, elections with the possibility of a second round, such as for governor and president of Brazil, would attract a larger number of candidates.

2.2 Factors that influence the vote

Voter behavior at the polls can be explained, based on political science, according to three theories: sociological, psychological and economic. The economic or racial theory indicates that citizens go to the polls for personal reasons, such as seeking well-being and an improvement in their economic situation. This behavior is the result of a low level of interest in politics, which means that little is spent on obtaining information on this subject (FIGUEIRA, 2013).

Figueira (2013) mentions that, in the sociological approach, unlike the previous one, the vote is the result of the voter's social context, linked mainly to interactions with the society in which they live and their political relationships. It can therefore be said that the difference between the two theories lies in the voter's decision. In economic theory, the voter acts rationally, taking into account their individual situation, while in sociological theory, the decision is based on a combination of their desires and the desires of the society in which they live. Figueira (2013) also mentions the psychological theory, which, according to the author, is based on low-information rationality, meaning that voters add to their political knowledge what is shown in election campaigns, in everyday life, in life experiences and in the relationships they have in society.

3 DATA MINING

The task of data mining is defined in various ways in the current literature. Among the definitions found, those considered most relevant have been highlighted.

Data mining offers the ability to view data in a new light, discovering previously undiscovered associations and patterns. Simply put, data mining is nothing more than the process of extracting new knowledge or unknown patterns from an existing data set (HAGOOD, 2012).

For Joseph, Sadath and Rajan (2013), data mining can be defined as a branch of computer science that deals with processing large data sets and discovering patterns in them. The main objective of data mining, according to the author, is to extract information and then transform it into a comprehensible structure that can be used in the future.

For Bacardit and Llorà (2013), a relevant fact to consider is that we are currently living in the *petabyte* era[3] , characterized by the huge generation of information. According to the author, we increasingly need to analyze, process and transform data. According to him, the use of robust data mining tools is necessary to achieve this goal.

Nowadays, the proliferation of information is also a fact of everyday life. Luiz *et al.* (2012) explains that this proliferation is mainly due to the great advances in computer technology, which increases the capacity for generating and storing data. The author also points out that the task of extracting knowledge from databases becomes unfeasible without the help of an appropriate data mining tool.

According to Sundar, Latha and Chandra (2012), the first studies on data mining appeared more than two decades ago, but its potential is only now being explored. For the author, data mining is the combination of statistical analysis, machine learning and database technology in order to extract patterns and relationships that were not previously noticed.

3.1 Knowledge discovery in databases

Knowledge discovery in databases, or KDD (*Knowledge Discovery Database*) can be defined as a non-trivial process of identifying new, potentially useful and ultimately understandable patterns in data (PADHY, MISHRA AND PANIGRAHI, 2012).

In order to perform the task of extracting knowledge from a database, it is necessary to follow a number of steps, including: selection, pre-processing, transformation, data mining (DM) and interpretation of the results. The data mining stage, specifically, can be divided into the tasks of classification, regression, association, *clustering* and *outlier* detection (LUIZ *ETAL.*, 2012).

3 Unit of data storage equivalent to 1024 terabytes, or 1,152,921,504,606,846,976 bytes (Digerati, 2009).

For Gupta, Kumar and Sharma (2011), the process of discovering knowledge in databases takes place in a different way, following these steps:

- Data cleaning: this is the phase where irrelevant data is removed;
- Data integration: in this stage multiple data sources, which can be heterogeneous, are combined into a single data set;
- Data selection: the moment when the data used for analysis is chosen from the data collection;
- Data transformation: phase also known as data consolidation, where the selected data is transformed into the appropriate format for the mining process;
- Data mining: this is the crucial step in the KDD process, where techniques are used to extract potentially useful patterns in the data;
- Evaluation of patterns: at this point in the process, the strictly interesting patterns are identified on the basis of previously indicated measures; and
- Knowledge representation: in the end, the knowledge discovered is represented visually for the user. In this phase, visualization techniques are used to help users understand and interpret the results of data mining.

3.2 Data mining techniques

Choosing the right method to mine the selected data is an important step towards achieving the desired knowledge. Among the various existing techniques, they can be classified as classic, such as: statistics, *clustering* and Nearest *Neighborhood*, and those of the new generation, which are decision trees, neural networks and association rules (JOSEPH, SADATH AND RAJAN, 2013).

3.2.1 Classification

According to Baradwaj and Pal (2011) classification is the most widely applied data mining technique today, which uses a set of pre-classified examples to create a model that can classify the population in general. This approach, according to the author, uses decision trees or neural network-based classification algorithms.

According to Groger, Niedermann and Mitschang (2012), decision trees can be considered a model whose main characteristic is its easy, understandable and intuitive interpretation due to its representation in the form of a tree (as shown in figure 1). Its structure is made up of nodes, or leaves, which represent a test, where each node is the result of that test, displaying a class label.

Figure 1 - Decision tree

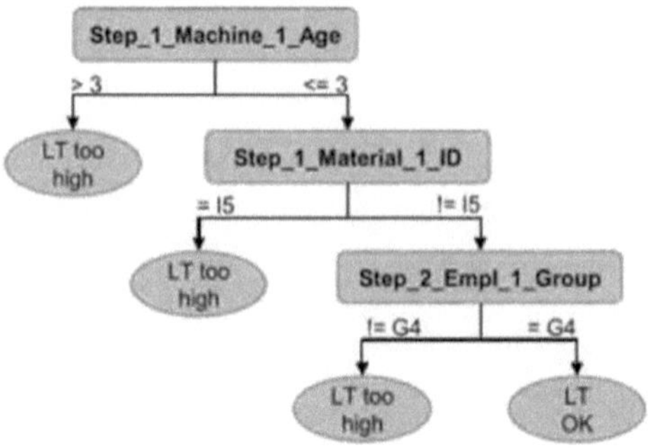

Source: Groger, Niedermann and Mitschang (2012)

3.2.2 J48 algorithm

The J48 algorithm was developed by *J Ross Quinlan,* and represents a version of the C4 algorithm (Kaur, Mohan and Sandhu, 2012). It uses two pruning methods[4] , the first of which is known as subtree replacement, i.e. the nodes of a decision tree can be replaced by a leaf, basically reducing the number of tests along a given path. The second type is called subtree capture. In this case, unlike the previous one, a node can be moved upwards towards the root of the tree, replacing the other nodes on the path (KAUR, MOHAN AND SANDHU, 2012).

According to Patil and Sherekar (2013), J48 is an algorithm that creates a simple binary decision tree. Below is the structure of the algorithm (figure 2), followed by a brief explanation by the author.

Figure 2 - J48 algorithm

3 The pruning process removes the branches that are not relevant to the classification model, selecting the sub-tree with the lowest estimated error rate (Oliveira, 2001).

```
Algoritmo J48:
ENTRADA:
        D //Dados de treinamento
SAÍDA
        T //Árvore de decisão
DTBUILD (*D)
{
T=ϕ; T= Cria nó raiz e rótulo com atributo de divisão;
T= Adiciona arc para o nó raiz para cada divisão de predicado e rótulo;
Para cada arc faz
        D= Banco de dados criado pela aplicação de divisão de predicado para D;
                Se o ponto de parada atingido por este caminho, então,
                        T'= cria o nó folha e rótulo com classe apropriada
                Se não
                        T'= DTBUILD(D);
                T= adiciona T' para arc;
}
```

Source: (Based on the algorithm presented by Patil and Sherekar, 2013)

During the construction of the tree, missing values are ignored, i.e. o value of an item can be predicted according to the attribute values for the other records. The aim is to divide the data into series, based on the attribute values for that item found in the sample (PATIL AND SHEREKAR, 2013).

In the process of building the J48 decision tree, whenever a set of items is found, the algorithm identifies the attribute that best discriminates between the various examples, i.e. among the possible values, if there is any value that is unambiguous, then that branch is closed and the value obtained is assigned to it (RAVICHANDRAN, SRINIVASAN AND RAMASAMY, 2012).

3.2.3 Association rules

Association rules play an important role in the task of data mining, their purpose is to find interesting associations, relationships or correlations in a large set of data items. In short, association rules show the conditions of occurrence of attribute values in a given data set (KUMAR AND CHADHA, 2012).

In different areas, according to Lee *et al.* (2013), association rules have gained great importance, including commerce, telecommunications, insurance and bioinformatics, helping the development of various corporations.

Association rules are defined by Shweta and Garg (2013) as statements that make relationships between data in a given database. According to the author, an association rule has two parts, one called antecedent, and the next, defined as consequent, for example, {egg} => {milk} (in this case egg is the antecedent and milk is the consequent), in which case the occurrence of the first item depends on the next item in the rule.

According to Angeline and James (2012), association rules were proposed by Agrawal *et al.* (1993), since then many algorithms for generating association rules have been created, among the most popular are Apriori, Eclat and FP-Growth.

3.2.4 Apriori algorithm

The Apriori algorithm was proposed by R. Agarwal and R. Srikant in 1994 with the aim of mining frequent item sets in databases using Boolean association rules (KUMARECHADHA, 2012).

According to Shweta and Garg (2013), Apriori is a word of Latin origin and its meaning is "with what comes first". According to the author, this type of algorithm uses a bottom-up strategy; it is considered the most famous and classic algorithm for mining frequent patterns.

3.3 Data mining tools

The task of data mining is made easier with the help of an appropriate tool. Among the various software available, two were chosen to be analyzed and learn more about their purposes, namely Weka (used in this work) and Rapidminer.

3.3.1 Rapidminer

Rapidminer, according to Costa *et al.* (2012), is a free and open source software, distributed independently for data analysis, allowing integration with other products developed by the same project. Some of the features highlighted by the author are:

- Free availability of the tool
- Works on most platforms
- Intuitive graphical interface
- Integration with different data sources

3.3.2 WEKA

The WEKA software is described by Nassif (2013) as a free tool, under the GPL *(Genaral Public License),* developed at the University of Waikato. According to the author, it was developed in Java and contains a graphical interface for interacting with data files and producing visual results (trees, curves and tables).

According to Hall *et al.* (2009), the WEKA tool has several graphical interfaces that allow easy access to its functionalities. The author also reports that the tool has, as its main interface, the "Explorer", where each panel represents a different data mining task, as well as a panel called "*Preprocess*", where the data sources are loaded and the attributes are selected.

4 DEVELOPMENT

This chapter will give details of the election data mining process, according to the proposed approach. This process aims to find classification rules, discovering patterns in the data presented, using *Data Mining* algorithms, through the WEKA software. Only mayoral candidate data was defined as a scope, thus allowing an analysis of all the municipalities in each state (as mentioned in the introduction section), without using such an extensive database, compared to the data for councillor candidates.

4.1 Procedures

This stage will show the procedures carried out to develop the proposed work. The origin of the data used and the format in which it is available will be presented, as well as the tools chosen to carry out the tasks that have been devised.

4.1.1 Data used

The data used in this study is provided free of charge by the Superior Electoral Court through the "Electoral Data Repository" portal (http://www.tse.jus.br/eleicoes/repositorio-de-dados-eleitorais), which is available for *download.* They are organized chronologically, allowing users to access data from municipal and national elections from 1994 to 2012.

This data is made available in compressed directories containing text files (in flat text format) for each federal unit. These files contain 1 (one) record per line and candidate data separated by semicolons (;), providing, for example, marital status, date of birth, party and result, in this case, whether or not the candidate was elected. In addition to candidate data for each election, you can access reports on electorate data.

In relation to the data mining proposal of this work, data was selected from the candidates for mayor of the states of Rio Grande do Sul, Sao Paulo, Bahia, Goias and Para, thus being able to evaluate the situation of all the regions of the country, each with its own social, cultural and financial characteristics. Below is a table showing the number of candidates per state and the total amount of data selected.

Table 1 - Data used

State	Total number of candidates	Mayoral candidates
Rio Grande do Sul	29052	1216
Sao Paulo	81622	2119
Bahia	36345	1206

Goias	20587	690
To	18780	504
Total	**186386**	**5735**

Source: Personal archive

In addition to the candidates' personal information, it is interesting to evaluate the importance that other data available in the aforementioned repository would have in the proposed knowledge discovery task, even if they are not in the aforementioned data set.

Among the data that has not been mentioned, those relating to the candidates' assets are also available. They are available in the same way as the candidates' registration data, i.e. stored in text files, one file for each federal unit, containing information on the candidates' assets that were declared before the election. These include the estimated value, type, description and, above all, a number that identifies the candidate who owns the asset.

From this data, it is possible to relate it to the candidates' registration data, generating, for example, the total assets of each individual, thus displaying a new attribute that can help in the intended data mining task, making it possible to assess how much this characteristic can influence the outcome of the election.

4.1.2 Tools used

The Microsoft Office Excel 2007 spreadsheet was used to process and filter the data, as it allows the data to be manipulated easily with the use of filtering mechanisms.

The data mining process proposed in this work depends on the use of appropriate algorithms. The following tool was used to support this task

WEKA (*Waikato Environment for Knowledge Analysis)*, which is available at http://sourceforge.net/projects/weka/?source=dlp. Other tools

4.2 Stages of development

The proposed data mining process consists of the following steps:

- Defining the scope
- Data selection
- Definition of attributes
- Data transformation
- Data mining
- Interpretation of results

- **.2.1Definition of scope**

After analyzing the data available on the TSE website, it was decided what scope should be adopted to carry out the proposed task. We therefore chose the data from the 2012 municipal elections in the states of Rio Grande do Sul, Sao Paulo, Bahia, Goias and Para.

After analyzing the available files, it was found that they contained data on candidates for mayor, deputy mayor and councillor, with approximately 30,000 records (in this case, data on candidates from the state of Rio Grande do Sul). As the aim is to analyze only one type of candidacy, only data relating to mayoral candidates was filtered out, which reduces the total number of records and, consequently, covers all the municipalities in the chosen states, getting to know the reality from small towns to state capitals.

- **.2.2 Data selection**

Once the scope to be studied has been defined, the next task is to filter and select the data, which is necessary because only the information relating to the mayoral candidates needs to be used.

Since the data was stored in text files, it had to be imported into a tool capable of carrying out the desired filtering. To do this, we chose *Microsoft*'s *Excel* 2007 spreadsheet, using the data import option (as shown in figure 3).

Figura 3 - Data import

Source: Personal archive

Once the data has been imported, the task of filtering the data is necessary, given that the imported file contains information on candidates for mayor, councillor and deputy mayor. To perform this task, we used the "filter" feature (as shown in figure 4), selecting only the "mayor" value.

Figura 4 - Filtering records

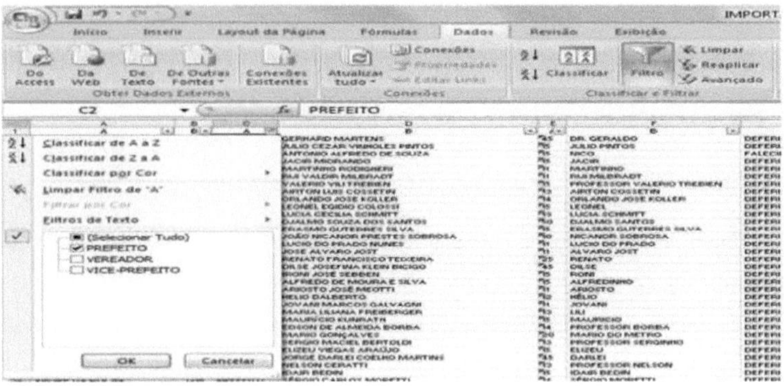

Source: Personal archive

4.2.3 Definition of attributes

After selecting the data, it was necessary to define which attributes would be used and which could be useful for achieving the proposed objective. The file available from the TSE contains 28 attributes, many of which are just information such as party, coalition, candidate name, among others, which were not considered important for what was proposed, as they are not linked to the candidates' personal characteristics.

Among the available attributes were selected:

- Date of birth
  - o Attribute referring to the candidate's date of birth, indicated in "day/month/year" format.
- Profession
  - o Profession of the candidate, informed before the election, described in full (teacher, dentist, veterinarian, etc.)
- Sex
  - o Candidate's gender (male or female)
- Higher Education
  - o Attribute that indicates whether or not the candidate has higher education.
- Marital status
  - o Marital status of the candidate before the election (married, single, divorced, etc).
- Campaign Expenses
  - o The candidate's total investment in the election campaign, represented by a numerical value.

- Birth City

o City where candidate was born or registered.

- Elected/Not elected

o The candidate's final standing in the election, indicating whether or not they were elected.

In choosing these attributes, it is important to note that the aim is to select only those that can bring some results, i.e. that can indicate some trend or pattern. Therefore, those attributes related to parties or coalitions were not considered relevant, as the main focus of the work is on the characteristics of the candidates.

4.2.4 Data transformation

During the first tests carried out on the WEKA tool, with the data that had been selected, it was observed that the results were not clear and the tool did not allow some algorithms to be executed, especially decision trees and association rules. The main reason is that the data was not properly formatted and organized. For example, the attribute that displays the date of birth has a wide range of values, which makes it difficult to process the data and understand the results.

Therefore, in order to make the most of the WEKA tool, some attributes were changed to reduce the variation in values by classifying the data into levels. It was then necessary to assign a scale to each one. Below are the changes that were made to the attributes mentioned.

- Date of birth:

o In this attribute it was necessary to change the representation of the values to age instead of date of birth. To do this, the candidate's age was calculated using the election date as a reference.

o After this change, the data was sorted as follows:

■ mHigh(71-80)

■ High(61-70)

■ Media(41-60)

■ Low(31-40)

■ mLow(18-30)

- Expenses

o Following the principle of the previous attribute, the data referring to campaign spending was classified in order to facilitate the data mining task. The classification was as follows:

- mHigh(>1Million)
- High (100mil-1mi)
- Average (10-100 thousand)
- Low(<10mil) }

In addition, other attributes have been standardized, allowing only the values "yes" and "no", as shown below.

- Profession => Politician { no,yes }

o Because this attribute has a wide range of values, it was decided to assign only the values "yes" or "no", identifying whether the candidate holds any political office (mayor, councillor, deputy, for example) during the campaign period.

- Marital status => Married { yes,no }

o This attribute has been standardized to only display whether the candidate's marital status is equal to "married". It allows the values "yes" and "no".

- City Birth = > CidNasc { no,yes }

o This attribute has already been set to "CidNasc", indicating whether or not the candidate was born in the city of candidacy. It also allows the values "yes" and "no". In this case, a formula has been created to check whether the attribute indicating the city of birth is the same as the attribute representing the city of candidacy.

- Higher Education

o This attribute has been changed to display only whether or not the candidate has a university degree.

After the changes, the table with the final data has the following composition, as shown in the image below (see figure 5).

Figura 5 - Final data

Político	Faixa de idade	Sexo	GrauInst	EnsSuperior	Casado	CidNasc	Total de bens	Despesa	Eleito
não	Alta(61-70)	M	7-SC	sim	sim	não	Medio(500mil-1mi)	Alta(100mil-1mi)	não
não	Alta(61-70)	M	7-SC	sim	não	sim	Baixo(100mil-500mil)	Alta(100mil-1mi)	sim
não	Media(41-60)	M	5-EMC	não	sim	não	Alto(1mi-50mi)	Alta(100mil-1mi)	não
não	Baixa(31-40)	M	7-SC	sim	sim	não	Alto(1mi-50mi)	Alta(100mil-1mi)	sim
não	Media(41-60)	M	7-SC	sim	sim	não	Baixo(100mil-500mil)	Média(10-100mil)	não
não	Media(41-60)	M	6-SI	não	sim	sim	Baixo(100mil-500mil)	Alta(100mil-1mi)	não
não	Media(41-60)	M	7-SC	sim	não	sim	mBaixo(<100mil)	Alta(100mil-1mi)	sim
não	Media(41-60)	M	6-SI	não	sim	não	Baixo(100mil-500mil)	Média(10-100mil)	sim
sim	Alta(61-70)	M	6-SI	não	sim	sim	Baixo(100mil-500mil)	Alta(100mil-1mi)	não
não	Media(41-60)	M	6-SI	não	sim	sim	Alto(1mi-50mi)	Média(10-100mil)	sim
não	Media(41-60)	F	7-SC	sim	não	sim	Baixo(100mil-500mil)	Média(10-100mil)	não
não	Media(41-60)	M	7-SC	sim	sim	não	Baixo(100mil-500mil)	Alta(100mil-1mi)	não
não	Media(41-60)	M	7-SC	sim	não	sim	Medio(500mil-1mi)	Alta(100mil-1mi)	sim
não	Alta(61-70)	M	7-SC	sim	sim	não	Baixo(100mil-500mil)	Alta(100mil-1mi)	não
não	mBaixa(18-30)	M	6-SI	não	sim	sim	Baixo(100mil-500mil)	Alta(100mil-1mi)	não
não	Media(41-60)	M	7-SC	sim	sim	não	Medio(500mil-1mi)	Alta(100mil-1mi)	não
não	Media(41-60)	M	3-EFC	não	sim	não	Baixo(100mil-500mil)	Alta(100mil-1mi)	sim
sim	Media(41-60)	F	7-SC	sim	sim	não	Baixo(100mil-500mil)	Alta(100mil-1mi)	não
sim	Media(41-60)	M	2-EFI	não	sim	não	mBaixo(<100mil)	Média(10-100mil)	sim
não	Alta(61-70)	M	5-EMC	não	sim	não	Baixo(100mil-500mil)	Média(10-100mil)	sim
não	Media(41-60)	M	7-SC	sim	sim	sim	mBaixo(<100mil)	Alta(100mil-1mi)	não

Once this stage had been completed, an XLS file (Excel 2003 spreadsheet format file) was created with only the data that would be used to carry out the data mining process. Once this file had been created, it was converted into the ARFF (Attribute-Relation File Format) format used by the WEKA tool.

The "Excel2Arff Converter" tool was used to carry out this conversion (as shown in figure 6).

Figura 6 - Excel2Arff Converter tool

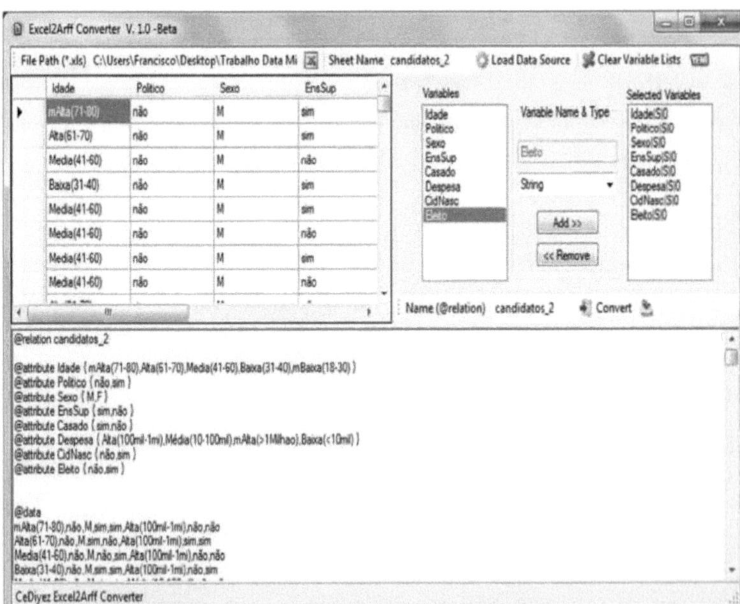

Source: Personal archive

Once the conversion had taken place, the file created had to be processed in the WEKA tool in order to obtain the desired results. Below is the main screen of the WEKA software, where the ARFF file was loaded and the preliminary information displayed (see figure 7).

Figure 7 - WEKA tool

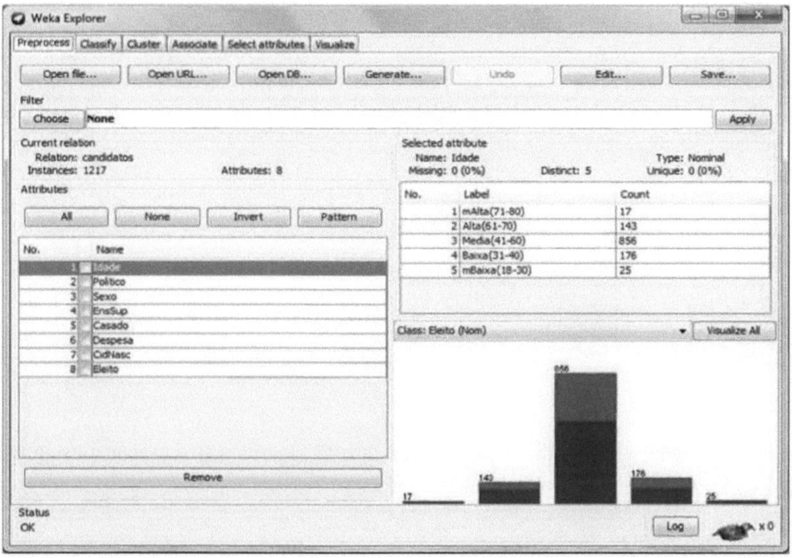

Source: Personal archive

4.2.5 Data mining

After filtering and selecting the data, it was uploaded to the WEKA tool to be submitted to the data mining algorithms. Among the various types of algorithms available in the tool, the J48 algorithm, of the classification type, was chosen because the decision trees (generated from this algorithm) are easy to understand. The results of mining the data from the municipal elections in the state of Rio Grande do Sul will be compared to the results obtained from the data from the municipal elections in Sao Paulo, Bahia, Goiâs and Parâ, identifying possible trends or differences.

After the data selection and filtering stages, it is necessary to use the chosen algorithms, using the WEKA tool, to generate the desired results. One of the algorithms chosen is J48, a decision tree algorithm. Figure 8 shows the screen where the algorithm and its settings are defined, as well as where the data mining is run and the result is displayed.

Figure 8 - J48 (decision tree)

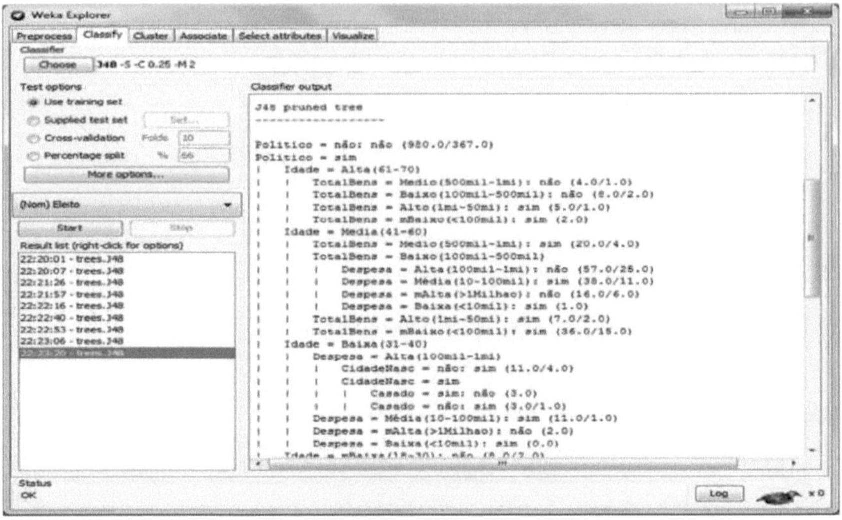

Source: Personal archive

After loading the data and selecting the J48 algorithm, the J48 algorithm was executed using the following *schema*:

- *weka.classifiers.trees.J48 -S -C 0.25 -M2*

Among the available attributes, those considered most relevant to obtaining the desired knowledge were selected, i.e. those that returned a more significant result (indicated by the higher percentage of correctly classified instances, shown in figure 11).

- Politics
- Age
- Higher Education
- Married
- CityBirth
- TotalGoods
- Expenses
- Elected

4.2.6 Results obtained

In order to fulfill the central objective of the work, the proposed data mining needs to be wide-ranging, thus being able to collect possible trends from different regions of Brazil, with their cultural, social and political characteristics. To this end, the data mining process was carried out by selecting just one federative unit from each region of Brazil, making the process smaller and easier. The criterion for selecting these states was the number of inhabitants, following the classification published in Portal Gl (2012), which mentions IBGE data from the same year (see table 2).

Table 2 - Population of Brazilian states

STATE	POPULATION
Southeast Region	
Sao Paulo	41.901.219
Minas Gerais	19.855.332
Rio de Janeiro	16.231.365
Holy Spirit	3.578.067
Northeast Region	
Bahia	14.175.341
Pernambuco	8.931.028
Ceara	8.606.005
Maranhao	6.714.314
Paraiba	3.815.171
Rio Grande do Norte	3.228.198
Alagoas	3.165.472
Piaui	3.160.748
Sergipe	2.110.867
Southern Region	
Rio Grande do Sul	10.770.603
Parana	10.577.755
Santa Catarina	6.383.286
Northern Region	
To	7.792.561
Amazonas	3.590.985
Rondonia	1.590.011
Tocantins	1.417.694
Acre	758.786
Amapa	698.602
Roraima	469.524
Central-West Region	
Goias	6.154.996
Mato Grosso	3.115.336
Federal District	2.648.532
Mato Grosso do Sul	2.505.088

Therefore, the following federal units were selected, covering the five regions of Brazil:

- Southern Region

o Rio Grande do Sul

- South East

o Sao Paulo

- North East

o Bahia

- Midwest

o Goias

- North

o To

Rio Grande do Sul

To start the process, data from the state of Rio Grande do Sul was selected. After loading this data into the tool and choosing the attributes involved in the process, the algorithm was run. Below is the header of the result shown (see figure 9).

Figure 9 - Execution information (Rio Grande do Sul)

```
=== Run information ===

Scheme:weka.classifiers.trees.J48 -S -C 0.25 -M 2
Relation:     dados-weka.filters.unsupervised.attribute.Remove-R3-4
Instances:    1216
Attributes:   8
              Politico
              Idade
              EnsSuperior
              Casado
              CidadeNasc
              TotalBens
              Despesa
              Eleito
Test mode:evaluate on training data
```

Source: Personal archive

This section of the result shows a summary of the mining process carried out, including:

- Scheme used: *weka.classifiers.trees.J48 -S-C 0.25 -M2*
- Number of attributes used: 8
- Number of records: 1216
- Test mode: *evaluate on training data*

After the result header, the decision tree is displayed, showing the relationship that each attribute had in the process carried out.

Figura 10- Decision tree (Rio Grande do Sul)

```
Politico = não: não (980.0/367.0)
Politico = sim
|   Idade = Alta(61-70)
|   |   TotalBens = Medio(500mil-1mi): não (4.0/1.0)
|   |   TotalBens = Baixo(100mil-500mil): não (8.0/2.0)
|   |   TotalBens = Alto(1mi-50mi): sim (5.0/1.0)
|   |   TotalBens = mBaixo(<100mil): sim (2.0)
|   Idade = Media(41-60)
|   |   TotalBens = Medio(500mil-1mi): sim (20.0/4.0)
|   |   TotalBens = Baixo(100mil-500mil)
|   |   |   Despesa = Alta(100mil-1mi): não (57.0/25.0)
|   |   |   Despesa = Média(10-100mil): sim (38.0/11.0)
|   |   |   Despesa = mAlta(>1Milhao): não (16.0/6.0)
|   |   |   Despesa = Baixa(<10mil): sim (1.0)
|   |   TotalBens = Alto(1mi-50mi): sim (7.0/2.0)
|   |   TotalBens = mBaixo(<100mil): sim (36.0/15.0)
|   Idade = Baixa(31-40)
|   |   Despesa = Alta(100mil-1mi)
|   |   |   CidadeNasc = não: sim (11.0/4.0)
|   |   |   CidadeNasc = sim
|   |   |   |   Casado = sim: não (3.0)
|   |   |   |   Casado = não: sim (3.0/1.0)
|   |   Despesa = Média(10-100mil): sim (11.0/1.0)
|   |   Despesa = mAlta(>1Milhao): não (2.0)
|   |   Despesa = Baixa(<10mil): sim (0.0)
|   Idade = mBaixa(18-30): não (8.0/2.0)
|   Idade = mAlta(71-80): não (4.0/1.0)

Number of Leaves  :     20

Size of the tree :      28
```

Source: Personal archive

You can see that the structure resembles a tree, where each value represents a relationship with the next value and each line a rule. In this case, the first line, or rule, contains the expression *"Politician= no: no (980.0/367.0)"*. This line indicates that in 980 records, when the politician attribute was equal to "no", the "elected" attribute resulted in "no" and in 367 records this rule does not apply, i.e. in 980 cases where the candidate did not hold an elective office before the election, they were not elected.

You can also see that there is a difference in the values compared to the first level, which indicates that the rules become more specific as the level of the tree changes. In addition, the more levels are advanced, the more restrictions the rule will have. For example, the rule

"*Expense = High(IOOmil-Imi): no (57.0/25.0)*" does not have only this element, but is formed as follows:

Politico= yes

Age = Average(41-60)

TotalAssets = Low(100mil-500mil)

Expenditure = High(100mil-1mi): no (57.0/25.0)

This rule indicates that the candidates who held political office, were between 41 and 60 years old, declared total assets of between 100 and 500 thousand reais, and invested between 100 thousand and 1 million reais in the campaign, 57 of whom were not elected. In 25 cases, this rule was not confirmed, i.e. it was not applied correctly.

After classifying the data, other results are presented (figures 11, 12 and 13), referring to the level of accuracy of the classification of the instances.

Figure 11- Summary (Rio Grande do Sul)

```
=== Summary ===

Correctly Classified Instances         773               63.5691 %
Incorrectly Classified Instances       443               36.4309 %
Kappa statistic                          0.153
Mean absolute error                      0.4572
Root mean squared error                  0.4781
Relative absolute error                 94.4663 %
Root relative squared error             97.1964 %
Total Number of Instances             1216
```

Source: Personal archive

In the result shown (figure 11), the item correctly *classified instances* indicates the number of correctly classified instances. The item "*Incorrectly classified instances*" indicates the number of incorrectly classified instances.

Figure 12 - Detailed accuracy by class (Rio Grande do Sul)

=== Detailed Accuracy By Class ===

	TP Rate	FP Rate	Precision	Recall	F-Measure	ROC Area	Class
	0.946	0.81	0.627	0.946	0.754	0.582	não
	0.19	0.054	0.709	0.19	0.3	0.582	sim
Weighted Avg.	0.636	0.5	0.66	0.636	0.568	0.582	

Source: Personal archive

Below these results, others are also displayed. In the case shown above (figure 12), the accuracy is displayed. According to Schwerz *et al.* (2013), accuracy can be defined as the quality of the classification of values, regardless of the class to which they belong; the closer the accuracy is to 1 (one), the closer the results will be to those previously known. The results obtained show that the accuracy of the "yes" and "no" values for the "elected" attribute are 0.709 and 0.627 respectively (as shown in figure 12).

Another important part of the result is the confusion matrix. According to Rovedder (2007), the confusion or error matrix is used to evaluate the result of a classification, displaying through a matrix, the number of instances classified correctly and incorrectly. In the data set analyzed, the following result was obtained, shown in figure 13.

Figura 13- Confusion matrix (Rio Grande do Sul)

```
=== Confusion Matrix ===

   a   b   <-- classified as
 678  39 |   a = não
 404  95 |   b = sim
```

Source: Personal archive

The diagonal of the matrix shows the total number of correctly classified instances for each item (a and b), i.e. 678 and 95, for a total of 773 records. The remaining values represent the incorrectly classified instances: 404 and 39, for a total of 443 records.

Sao Paulo

After mining the electoral data of candidates from Rio Grande do Sul, the same process was carried out with the data of candidates from the state of Sao Paulo, using the same parameters mentioned above and selecting the same attributes, resulting in the following decision tree, shown in figure 14.

Figura 14- - Decision tree (Sao Paulo)

```
Politico = não: não (1757.0/492.0)
Politico = sim
|   Despesa = Alta(100mil-1mi)
|   |   TotalBens = mBaixo(<100mil): não (163.0/62.0)
|   |   TotalBens = Baixo(100mil-500mil): sim (43.0/21.0)
|   |   TotalBens = Alto(1mi-50mi): sim (5.0/1.0)
|   |   TotalBens = Medio(500mil-1mi)
|   |   |   Casado = sim
|   |   |   |   EnsSuperior = sim: não (3.0/1.0)
|   |   |   |   EnsSuperior = não: sim (7.0)
|   |   |   Casado = não: não (2.0)
|   Despesa = Média(10-100mil)
|   |   TotalBens = mBaixo(<100mil)
|   |   |   Idade = Baixa(31-40): não (2.0/1.0)
|   |   |   Idade = Media(41-60): sim (21.0/5.0)
|   |   |   Idade = mAlta(71-80): sim (0.0)
|   |   |   Idade = Alta(61-70): não (4.0/1.0)
|   |   |   Idade = mBaixa(18-30): sim (0.0)
|   |   TotalBens = Baixo(100mil-500mil): não (9.0/3.0)
|   |   TotalBens = Alto(1mi-50mi): sim (1.0)
|   |   TotalBens = Medio(500mil-1mi): sim (1.0)
|   Despesa = Baixa(<10mil)
|   |   Idade = Baixa(31-40): sim (2.0)
|   |   Idade = Media(41-60): não (3.0/1.0)
|   |   Idade = mAlta(71-80): sim (0.0)
|   |   Idade = Alta(61-70): sim (0.0)
|   |   Idade = mBaixa(18-30): sim (0.0)
|   Despesa = mAlta(>1Milhao): não (96.0/29.0)

Number of Leaves  :     21

Size of the tree :      29
```

Source: Personal archive

It can be seen that the resulting tree shows some differences from the previous tree, which refers to electoral data from Rio Grande do Sul. On the other hand, a similarity can be observed: the "*politician*" attribute is also at the top of the tree. As the result shows, in 1757 records, when the attribute was equal to "no", the elected attribute had the value "no", i.e. in almost all cases this rule was applied correctly, confirming in yet another scenario the importance of this factor in the choice of candidate.

Another prominent attribute is "expenditure", which indicates how much each candidate has invested in the political campaign. In the result obtained, it can be seen that this attribute is just below the "politician" attribute, ranking second, which indicates its importance in data classification. In addition to the decision tree, the summary was generated, showing a summary of the information (see figure 15).

Figure 15- Summary (São Paulo)

```
=== Summary ===

Correctly Classified Instances        1502               70.8825 %
Incorrectly Classified Instances       617               29.1175 %
Kappa statistic                          0.0852
Mean absolute error                      0.4085
Root mean squared error                  0.4519
Relative absolute error                 96.6204 %
Root relative squared error             98.3041 %
Total Number of Instances             2119
```

Source: Personal archive

This section of the result shows that approximately 70% of the instances were correctly classified and 29% were incorrectly classified. Another important part of the result is the table showing the accuracy factor of the algorithm used, as shown in figure 16.

Figure 16- Detailed accuracy by class (Sao Paulo)

```
=== Detailed Accuracy By Class ===

               TP Rate   FP Rate   Precision   Recall  F-Measure   ROC Area  Class
                 0.982     0.918     0.711      0.982     0.824      0.552    não
                 0.082     0.018     0.663      0.082     0.147      0.552    sim
Weighted Avg.    0.709     0.645     0.696      0.709     0.619      0.552
```

Source: Personal archive

Note that the algorithm's accuracy for the "no" value of the "elected" attribute was 0.711. For the "yes" value, it was 0.663.

Another important part of the result is the confusion matrix. In this analysis, the following matrix was generated, shown in figure 17.

Figure 17- Confusion matrix (Sao Paulo)

```
=== Confusion Matrix ===

    a    b   <-- classified as
 1449   27 |   a = não
  590   53 |   b = sim
```

Source: Personal archive

It can be said that the total number of instances classified correctly was 1502 (sum of the values 1449 and 53), while the total number of instances classified incorrectly was 617 (sum of the remaining values).

Bahia

After mining the data from two states, one in the south and the other in the southeast, it became interesting to analyze the data from other regions of Brazil. The region chosen in this case is the northeast, represented by the state of Bahia, which has the largest number of inhabitants in the region.

After loading the data into the WEKA tool, the J48 algorithm was selected, its parameters were set and it was run. After running the algorithm, a decision tree was generated, which has the following header, as shown in the figure below.

Figura 18- Execution information (Bahia)

```
=== Run information ===

Scheme:weka.classifiers.trees.J48 -S -C 0.4 -M 2
Relation:     dados-weka.filters.unsupervised.attribute.Remove-R3-4
Instances:    1206
Attributes:   8
              Politico
              Idade
              EnsSuperior
              Casado
              CidadeNasc
              TotalBens
              Despesa
              Eleito
Test mode:evaluate on training data

=== Classifier model (full training set) ===
```

Source: Personal archive

The header displays the following main items of information:

- Scheme: weka.classifiers.trees.J48 -S -C 0.4 -M 2

o Unlike the previous analyses, in this case the confidence factor was increased from 0.25 (the tool's default value) to 0.4. This change was made due to the constraints of the previously proposed scheme. With the value set at 0.25, the algorithm performed the pruning process more drastically on the analyzed data, not returning the decision tree. Increasing the confidence value to 0.4 caused the tree to be

displayed. According to Silva (2007), lower confidence levels tend to penalize classification involving a smaller number of records.

- Number of instances: 1206

o Total number of records in the *dataset* used, corresponding to the number of candidates.

- Nº of attributes used: 8

- Classification model selected: *full training set*

After the result header, the tree itself is displayed, showing the rules that have been generated. It has the following structure, as shown in figure 19.

Figure 19- Decision tree (Bahia)

```
Despesa = Alta(100mil-1mi)
|   Politico = não: não (836.0/290.0)
|   Politico = sim
|   |   TotalBens = Medio(500mil-1mi): sim (18.0/7.0)
|   |   TotalBens = Alto(1mi-50mi)
|   |   |   Casado = sim: não (13.0/2.0)
|   |   |   Casado = não: sim (5.0/2.0)
|   |   TotalBens = mBaixo(<100mil)
|   |   |   EnsSuperior = sim: não (17.0/7.0)
|   |   |   EnsSuperior = não
|   |   |   |   Casado = sim: sim (23.0/8.0)
|   |   |   |   Casado = não: não (15.0/6.0)
|   |   TotalBens = Baixo(100mil-500mil)
|   |   |   Idade = Media(41-60)
|   |   |   |   CidadeNasc = não: não (34.0/13.0)
|   |   |   |   CidadeNasc = sim
|   |   |   |   |   Casado = sim: sim (23.0/10.0)
|   |   |   |   |   Casado = não: não (4.0/1.0)
|   |   |   Idade = Baixa(31-40)
|   |   |   |   CidadeNasc = não: sim (6.0/2.0)
|   |   |   |   CidadeNasc = sim: não (6.0/2.0)
|   |   |   Idade = mBaixa(18-30): sim (1.0)
|   |   |   Idade = Alta(61-70)
|   |   |   |   EnsSuperior = sim: sim (7.0/2.0)
|   |   |   |   EnsSuperior = não: não (3.0/1.0)
|   |   |   Idade = mAlta(71-80): sim (1.0)
Despesa = mAlta(>1Milhao)
|   TotalBens = Medio(500mil-1mi): não (20.0/4.0)
|   TotalBens = Alto(1mi-50mi)
|   |   EnsSuperior = sim: não (18.0/4.0)
|   |   EnsSuperior = não: sim (7.0/2.0)
|   TotalBens = mBaixo(<100mil): não (18.0/1.0)
|   TotalBens = Baixo(100mil-500mil)
|   |   Politico = não
|   |   |   CidadeNasc = não: sim (13.0/5.0)
|   |   |   CidadeNasc = sim: não (9.0/1.0)
|   |   Politico = sim: sim (9.0/3.0)
Despesa = Média(10-100mil): não (86.0/11.0)
Despesa = Baixa(<10mil): não (14.0/3.0)

Number of Leaves  :     25

Size of the tree :      40
```

Source: Personal archive

The main difference with previous trees is the position of the attributes in the tree. For example, the "expenditure" attribute is at the top of the tree and on the first level, unlike the previous cases, where the "politician" attribute was in this position.

In relation to the "expenditure" attribute, the values "High(lOOmil-lmi)" and "mHigh(>lMillion)" had a greater number of records than the other values in the series, indicating a possible influence of the value of the campaign investment on the final result of the municipal elections in the state of Bahia.

In the result summary, the following information was displayed, as shown in figure 2O.

Figura 20 - Summary (Bahia)

```
=== Summary ===

Correctly Classified Instances         819               67.9104 %
Incorrectly Classified Instances       387               32.0896 %
Kappa statistic                          0.1451
Mean absolute error                      0.4234
Root mean squared error                  0.4601
Relative absolute error                 93.4592 %
Root relative squared error             96.6826 %
Total Number of Instances             1206
```

Source: Personal archive

In this summary, it can be seen that the correctly classified instances correspond to 8l9 (67.9%), and the incorrectly classified instances amount to 387 (32.8%). After the summary, an analysis of the procedure's accuracy is displayed (see figure 2l).

figura 21 Detailed accuracy by class (Bahia)

=== Detailed Accuracy By Class ===

	TP Rate	FP Rate	Precision	Recall	F-Measure	ROC Area	Class
	0.948	0.828	0.683	0.948	0.794	0.617	não
	0.172	0.052	0.637	0.172	0.271	0.617	sim
Weighted Avg.	0.679	0.559	0.667	0.679	0.613	0.617	

Source: Personal archive

The accuracy for the "no" value of the chosen attribute was 0.683, while the accuracy for the "yes" value was 0.637. With regard to the confusion matrix, the result was similar to the other cases.

Figure 22 - Confusion matrix (Bahia)

```
=== Confusion Matrix ===

   a   b   <-- classified as
 747  41 |   a = não
 346  72 |   b = sim
```

Source: Personal archive

You can see that the instances classified correctly are 747 and 72, while those classified incorrectly are 41 and 346.

Goias

Following the objective of the proposed work, and after analyzing the data from the states already mentioned, it is necessary to analyze one state in the north and one in the central-west, thus covering the 5 (five) regions of Brazil. The next state analyzed has a smaller number of candidates, which may generate different results from the previous ones, making it interesting to compare the results presented.

Therefore, after loading the file containing the data into the WEKA tool and running the J48 algorithm, the result was generated, with the following header (see figure 23).

Figura 23 - Execution info (Goias)

```
=== Run information ===

Scheme:weka.classifiers.trees.J48 -S -C 0.4 -M 2
Relation:     dados-weka.filters.unsupervised.attribute.Remove-R3-4
Instances:    690
Attributes:   8
              Politico
              Idade
              EnsSuperior
              Casado
              CidadeNasc
              TotalBens
              Despesa
              Eleito
Test mode:evaluate on training data
```

Source: Personal archive

This header is made up of the following information:

- Schema: weka.classifiers.trees.J48 -S -C 0.4 -M 2

o For this data set, the same scheme was used as for the data from the state of Bahia.

- Instances: 690
- Attributes used: 8
- Test mode: *Training data*

After the header comes the decision tree resulting from the process, which has the following structure, as shown in the figure below (figure 24).

Figura 24 - Execution tree (Goiás)

```
Despesa = mAlta(>1Milhao)
|   Idade = Media(41-60): não (61.0/19.0)
|   Idade = Alta(61-70): sim (13.0/4.0)
|   Idade = Baixa(31-40): não (23.0/5.0)
|   Idade = mBaixa(18-30): não (3.0/1.0)
|   Idade = mAlta(71-80): não (0.0)
Despesa = Média(10-100mil): não (26.0/5.0)
Despesa = Alta(100mil-1mi)
|   Casado = sim
|   |   TotalBens = Baixo(100mil-500mil)
|   |   |   Idade = Media(41-60)
|   |   |   |   Politico = sim
|   |   |   |   |   EnsSuperior = sim
|   |   |   |   |   |   CidadeNasc = não: sim (6.0/1.0)
|   |   |   |   |   |   CidadeNasc = sim: não (2.0)
|   |   |   |   |   EnsSuperior = não: não (17.0/5.0)
|   |   |   |   Politico = não: não (92.0/34.0)
|   |   |   Idade = Alta(61-70): não (21.0/7.0)
|   |   |   Idade = Baixa(31-40): não (34.0/16.0)
|   |   |   Idade = mBaixa(18-30): sim (3.0)
|   |   |   Idade = mAlta(71-80): não (0.0)
|   |   TotalBens = Alto(1mi-50mi): não (97.0/38.0)
|   |   TotalBens = Medio(500mil-1mi)
|   |   |   Idade = Media(41-60)
|   |   |   |   EnsSuperior = sim: sim (22.0/8.0)
|   |   |   |   EnsSuperior = não
|   |   |   |   |   Politico = sim: sim (7.0/3.0)
|   |   |   |   |   Politico = não: não (29.0/13.0)
|   |   |   Idade = Alta(61-70): não (4.0)
|   |   |   Idade = Baixa(31-40): sim (4.0/1.0)
|   |   |   Idade = mBaixa(18-30): sim (0.0)
|   |   |   Idade = mAlta(71-80): não (1.0)
|   |   TotalBens = mBaixo(<100mil)
|   |   |   Politico = sim
|   |   |   |   Idade = Media(41-60): não (11.0/4.0)
|   |   |   |   Idade = Alta(61-70): sim (1.0)
|   |   |   |   Idade = Baixa(31-40): sim (4.0/1.0)
|   |   |   |   Idade = mBaixa(18-30): sim (0.0)
|   |   |   |   Idade = mAlta(71-80): sim (0.0)
|   |   |   Politico = não: não (68.0/19.0)
|   |   TotalBens = mAlto(>50milhoes): não (0.0)
|   Casado = não: não (132.0/37.0)
Despesa = Baixa(<10mil): não (9.0)

Number of Leaves  :     31

Size of the tree :      44
```

Source: Personal archive

As with the results for the state of Bahia, the expenditure attribute also featured prominently in the decision tree, in this case ranking above attributes such as "Age", "Total Assets" and others. Another factor observed is that the "politician" attribute, which was very important in the results presented from the data for the states of Sao Paulo and Rio Grande do Sul, was not at the top of the tree in the state of Goiás, ranking below attributes such as "Age" and "Higher Education". After analyzing the tree, we need to check the summary of the result, which is shown in figure 25.

Figure 25 - Summary (Goias)

```
=== Summary ===

Correctly Classified Instances         424               61.4493 %
Incorrectly Classified Instances       266               38.5507 %
Kappa statistic                         -0.0038
Mean absolute error                      0.4521
Root mean squared error                  0.4909
Relative absolute error                 98.6871 %
Root relative squared error            102.5757 %
Total Number of Instances              690
```

Source: Personal archive

It can be seen that of 690 instances, 424 were classified correctly and 266 incorrectly, resulting in percentages of 61.4% and 38.5% respectively.

With regard to the accuracy of the values of the chosen attribute, the result showed an accuracy of 0.348 for the "yes" value and 0.644 for the "no" value, as can be seen in figure 26.

Figura 26 - Detailed accuracy by class (Goiâs)

```
=== Detailed Accuracy By Class ===

               TP Rate   FP Rate   Precision   Recall  F-Measure   ROC Area  Class
                 0.098     0.101      0.348     0.098     0.153      0.528    sim
                 0.899     0.902      0.644     0.899     0.75       0.528    não
Weighted Avg.    0.614     0.618      0.539     0.614     0.538      0.528
```

Source: Personal archive

In addition, the confusion matrix had a different distribution compared to the previous results, as can be seen in figure 27.

Figura 27 - Matriz de confusao (Goias)

```
=== Confusion Matrix ===

  a   b   <-- classified as
 24 221 |   a = sim
 45 400 |   b = não
```

Source: Personal archive

In this case, the highest values were in column b, i.e. referring to the value "no", while in column "b" the values were lower. The records classified correctly are 24 and 400 (totaling 424) and those classified incorrectly are 45 and 221 (totaling 266).

To

After mining the electoral data from the states of Rio Grande do Sul, Sao Paulo, Bahia and Goias, from the south, southeast, northeast and central-west regions, respectively, all that remained was to mine the data from a state in the northern region of Brazil, completing what was initially proposed. The state of Para was then selected as the target. Therefore, after loading the selected data into the WEKA tool, the J48 algorithm was run, with the following parameters shown in the figure below.

Figura 28 - Execution information (To)

```
=== Run information ===

Scheme:weka.classifiers.trees.J48 -S -C 0.4 -M 2
Relation:     dados-weka.filters.unsupervised.attribute.Remove-R3-4
Instances:    504
Attributes:   8
              Politico
              Idade
              EnsSuperior
              Casado
              CidadeNasc
              TotalBens
              Despesa
              Eleito
Test mode:evaluate on training data
```

Source: Personal archive

The parameters displayed include:

- Scheme: weka.classifiers.trees.J48 -S -C 0.4 -M 2

o The same scheme was used for the states of Bahia and Goiás, due to the characteristics of the data set.

- Instances: 504

o Total registrations used, i.e. total mayoral candidates.

- Attributes used: 8

o Set the same attributes as in the previous cases.

- Test mode: *evaluate on training data*

Based on these parameters, the algorithm is run, generating the following decision tree, as shown in the image below.

Figure 29 - Decision tree (Parâ)

```
J48 pruned tree
------------------

Politico = sim
|   Idade = Media(41-60)
|   |   EnsSuperior = sim
|   |   |   TotalBens = mBaixo(<100mil): sim (3.0)
|   |   |   TotalBens = Baixo(100mil-500mil): não (9.0/3.0)
|   |   |   TotalBens = Medio(500mil-1mi): sim (5.0/2.0)
|   |   |   TotalBens = Alto(1mi-50mi)
|   |   |   |   Despesa = mAlta(>1Milhao): não (2.0)
|   |   |   |   Despesa = Alta(100mil-1mi): sim (3.0/1.0)
|   |   |   |   Despesa = Média(10-100mil): não (0.0)
|   |   |   |   Despesa = Baixa(<10mil): não (0.0)
|   |   |   TotalBens = mAlto(>50milhoes): sim (0.0)
|   |   EnsSuperior = não: não (50.0/16.0)
|   Idade = Alta(61-70): sim (7.0/2.0)
|   Idade = Baixa(31-40): não (18.0/5.0)
|   Idade = mBaixa(18-30): sim (2.0)
|   Idade = mAlta(71-80): não (1.0)
Politico = não: não (404.0/103.0)
```

Source: Personal archive

The first thing to notice about this tree is its structure, which is much smaller compared to the other trees generated in this work. The position of the attributes is another important aspect. As in the tree generated from the Rio Grande do Sul data, the attributes "politician" and "age" are above the other attributes.

Another attribute that can be highlighted is "Higher Education". This is located just below the age attribute, making it important for classifying data.

With regard to the level of accuracy in classifying the data, the proportion was closer to the previous cases, with 73.8% of instances classified correctly and 26.19% classified incorrectly, but slightly higher than the others, as can be seen in figure 30.

Figure 30 - Summary (To)

```
=== Summary ===

Correctly Classified Instances        372               73.8095 %
Incorrectly Classified Instances      132               26.1905 %
Kappa statistic                          0.1243
Mean absolute error                      0.383
Root mean squared error                  0.4376
Relative absolute error                 94.5532 %
Root relative squared error             97.2835 %
Total Number of Instances              504
```

Source: Personal archive

Regarding the algorithm's accuracy for the values of the "elected" attribute, there was some approximation. For the value "yes" the accuracy was 0.75 and for the value "no" it was 0.738, as can be seen in figure 31.

Figure 31- Detailed accuracy by class (Para)

=== Detailed Accuracy By Class ===

	TP Rate	FP Rate	Precision	Recall	F-Measure	ROC Area	Class
	0.106	0.014	0.75	0.106	0.185	0.568	sim
	0.986	0.894	0.738	0.986	0.844	0.568	não
Weighted Avg.	0.738	0.646	0.741	0.738	0.658	0.568	

Source: Personal archive

In the confusion matrix, as in the previous case, there was a certain difference in the distribution of values, with the highest values being in column B. In relation to the correctly classified records, the values of 15 and 357 were displayed, as shown in figure 32.

Figure 32 - Confusion matrix (Para)

```
=== Confusion Matrix ===

  a   b   <-- classified as
 15 127 |   a = sim
  5 357 |   b = não
```

Source: Personal archive

4.2.7 Interpreting the results

It was possible to observe several important aspects from the results generated, both in terms of the rules generated and the resulting numbers and percentages.

In relation to the numbers generated, we can observe some aspects that are useful for analyzing the efficiency of the J48 algorithm, as well as possible relationships between these results.

By analyzing the results presented and the total number of inhabitants in each state (figure 33), it is possible to make a comparison between these data.

Figura 33 - Population of the states analyzed

Source: Personal archive

Figure 33 shows the total number of inhabitants per state, based on IBGE data for 2012 (see section 3.2.2, page 32), published by the Gl portal (2012). Figure 34 shows the total number of instances or records for each selected state.

Figura 34 - Total registrations (candidates)

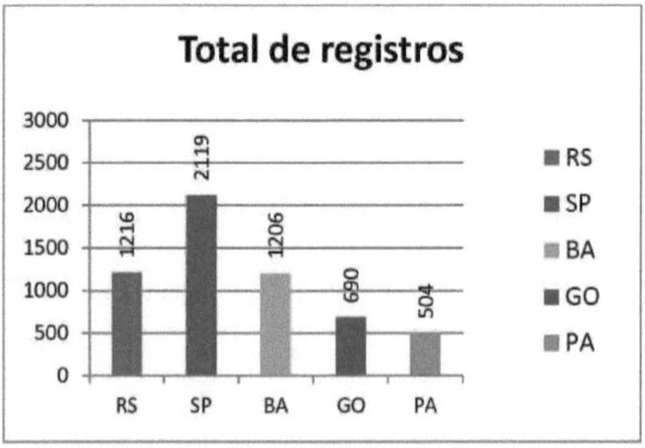

Source: Personal archive

Looking at these graphs, it can be said that there was a certain similarity between the population of each state (figure 33) and the number of instances (figure 34), i.e. the total number of mayoral candidates. For example, Sao Paulo, the most populous state, is the one that had the most instances to be analyzed.

As for the size of the tree generated (see figure 35), there was no relation to the size of the population, because as can be seen for the data from the state of Goiás, the least populous, the tool generated a tree with 31 levels and 44 lines, the largest generated in the study.

Figure 35- Tree size

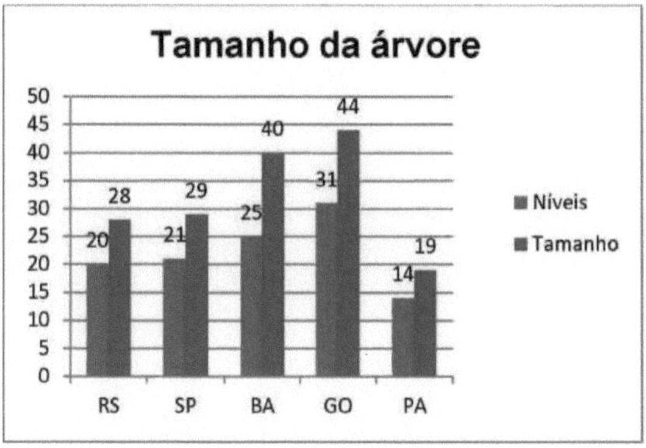

Source: Personal archive

In relation to the algorithm's accuracy, other aspects can be verified, as can be seen in the graphs below (figure 36 and 37).

Figura 36- Hits per instance

Source: Personal archive

This graph (figure 36) shows that the instances classified correctly are always higher than the instances classified incorrectly. In some cases, the total of correct classifications is well above the incorrect ones, as is the case in the states of Sao Paulo and Bahia, for example.

Figure 37 shows the level of accuracy per class for each state chosen.

Figura 37- Hit level per class

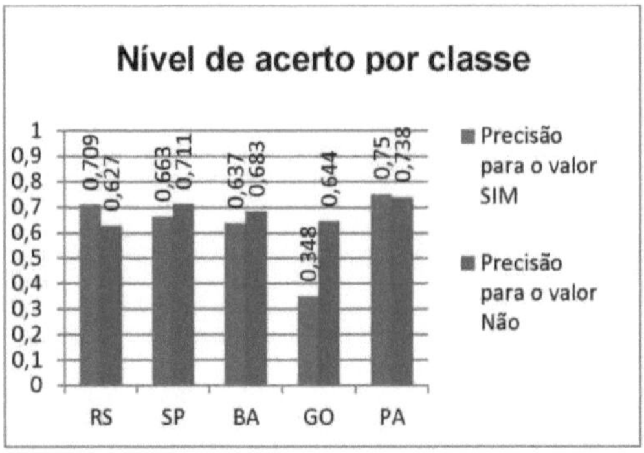

Source: Personal archive

It can be seen that the algorithm's accuracy for o values "yes" (elected) and "no" (not elected) in most cases was similar (as can be seen in figure 37), resulting in little difference. Except for the state of Goias, where the accuracy for the "yes" value was much lower than the accuracy for the "no" value.

With regard to the rules generated, the main focus of the work, it was possible to observe many similarities between the results. Some attributes were more important in classifying the data, making them important for identifying trends or patterns between states.

Among these attributes, the most important was "Politician", which indicates whether the candidate held or had held elective public office before the 2012 election. Among the five states analyzed, in three of them this attribute was at the top of the tree, indicating the importance of this factor in the choice of candidate, i.e. political experience directly influences the voter's choice at the polls. An example is the tree generated from the data for the state of Rio Grande do Sul, where the first rule displays: "Politico=nao: nao (980.0/ 367.0)". This rule indicates that, in 980 records, candidates who did not hold political office were not elected. In 367 records, this rule does not apply correctly.

The "Expenditure" attribute can also be considered another highlight in the results. In two of the trees generated, referring to data from Goias and Bahia, it was at the top, and in the tree generated from data from the state of Sao Paulo, the attribute was just below the "political" attribute, indicating its importance for classifying the data.

With regard to the rules displayed for this attribute, those indicating greater campaign spending resulted in a greater number of correctly classified records favoring the election of the candidates. Values indicating little campaign spending, on the other hand, indicated a negative trend in relation to the election of candidates. For example, in the trees generated from data from the states of Goias and Bahia, the rule for the value "Low(<10,000)", which indicates that the candidate invested less than 10,000 reais in the campaign, did not indicate the likelihood of the candidate being elected.

It can also be said that the age of the candidate is another important factor observed in the results obtained. In three states, Bahia, Goias and Rio Grande do Sul, the "Age" attribute was just below the first attribute in the decision tree. Analyzing the results, it is possible to see a tendency for candidates with low ages (between 18 and 30) and advanced ages (between 71 and 80) not to be elected.

In addition to the attributes already mentioned, others also had an influence on the final result, including the "TotalAssets" attribute, which indicates the candidate's total assets. Other attributes did not have as much influence on the result. These include "Higher Education", "Married" and "CidNasc".

5 METHODOLOGY

In order to construct this work, it was necessary to go through a number of stages, which were considered important in order to achieve what was proposed. The first step, with the central theme of the work in mind, was to research the theoretical framework, which was necessary in order to have a basis for developing the next steps.

Among the core topics researched was data mining, including classification techniques. In addition to this topic, knowledge discovery in databases was also researched, as well as a brief reference on the main data mining tools, including WEKA.

In addition to the above, another important topic is the political situation in Brazil, where the work is based. Important aspects of current Brazilian politics were mentioned, including a brief history. Another relevant factor for this work is to identify the objectives and expectations of voters at the time of voting, in other words, the profile of each voter and what motivates their choice of candidates.

After acquiring a theoretical basis, the first steps in the development of the work were taken. One of these steps was to define the scope of the study, i.e. which data source would be used to carry out the data mining process. To do this, a brief selection and filtering of the available data was carried out, selecting only those considered useful for the proposed work.

In order to carry out this important development step, it was necessary to define which tool would be responsible for extracting the desired knowledge. In addition, it was determined which methods and algorithms would be used in this procedure.

Once the data had been mined, the results were generated and analyzed in order to discover probable patterns and trends that could be observed.

6 CONCLUSION

When a voter experiences an election period, many thoughts come to the surface, a lot of information is provided and many ideas are formed about the candidates. These ideas are influenced in various ways, both by the group in which one lives, by the people who participate in the citizen's daily life and, increasingly, by the media, which is decisive in bringing the characteristics of each candidate to the attention of the people. This study allowed us to find out how decisive these characteristics are in the outcome of an election. The results showed that, above all, factors such as political experience, campaign spending and age were important in classifying the data. Until the final stage of the work was reached, many challenges were encountered. Among them, the task of selecting and filtering the data, mainly due to the quantity and characteristics of the data available, was the main challenge, as it was necessary to find the right format for the data in order to get the best use out of the data mining tool. In view of the difficulties presented and the results obtained, it can be said that the objectives were achieved and it was possible to obtain the idealized knowledge. For future work, it would be interesting to evaluate the patterns found by comparing them with other electoral periods, and to compare them with data from the following elections or with previous elections.

7 REFERENCES

AGRAWAL, R.; FALOUTSOS, C.; SWAMI, A. Efficient similarity search in sequence databases. **Proceedings of the 4th International Conference of Foundations of Data Organization and Algorithms (FODO)**, 1993.

ANGELINE, D. M. D.; JAMES, I. S. P. Association Rule Generation Using Apriori Mend Algorithm for Student ' s Placement. **Int. J. Emerg. Sci.**, v. 2, n. March, p. 78-86, 2012.

BACARDIT, J.; LLORÀ, X. Large-scale data mining using genetics-based machine learning.

Wiley Interdisciplinary Reviews: Data Mining and Knowledge Discovery, v. 3, n. 1, p. 37-61, 9jan. 2013.

BARADWAJ, B. K.; PAL, S. Mining Educational Data to Analyze Students " Performance. **International Journal of Advanced Computer Science and Applications**, v. 2, n. 6, p. 6369, 2011.

COSTA, E. *étal.* Educational Data Mining: Concepts, Techniques, Tools and Applications. v. d, p. 1-29, 2012.

DIGERATI, E. **Hardware for professionals**. [s.l.] Digerati Books, 2009. p. 128

FELISBINO, R. DE A.; BERNABEL, R. T.; KERBAUY, M. T. M. Only one should win: the recruitment bases of mayoral candidates in Brazilian capitals in 2008. **Revista de Sociologia e Politica**, v. 21, n. 41, p. 219-234, 2012.

FIGUEIRA, P. R. Effects of virtual campaigning in the social media universe: voter behavior on Twitter in the 2010 Elections. **Revista Compolitica**, v. 1, n. 3, p. 826, 2013.

G1, P. **Brazil has 193,946,886 inhabitants, according to IBGE estimate**. Available at:< http://g1.globo.com/brasil/noticia/2012/08/brasil-tem-193946886-habitantes-aponta- estimativa-do-ibge.html> Accessed on: 15jul. 2013.

GAXIE, D. The logics of political recruitment. **Revista Brasileira de Ciència Politica**, n. 8, p. 165-208, 2012.

GROGER, C.; NIEDERMANN, F.; MITSCHANG, B. Data Mining-driven Manufacturing Process Optimization. **Proceedings of the World Congress on Engineering**, v. III, p. 0-6, 2012.

GUPTA, S.; KUMAR, D.; SHARMA, A. DATA MINING CLASSIFICATION TECHNIQUES APPLIED FOR BREAST CANCER DIAGNOSIS AND PROGNOSIS.

Journal of Computer Science, v. 2, n. 2, p. 188-195, 2011.

HAGOOD, J. A Brief Introduction to Data Mining Projects in the Humanities. **Bulletin of the**

American Society for Information Science and Technology, v. 38, n. 4, p. 20-23, 2012.

HALL, M. *et al.* The WEKA Data Mining Software : An Update. **SIGKDD Explorations**, v. 11,n. 1,p. 10-18, 2009.

JOSEPH, M. V; SADATH, L.; RAJAN, V. Data Mining : A Comparative Study on Various Techniques and Methods. **International Journal of Advanced Research in Computer Science and Software Engineering**, v. 3, n. 2, p. 106-113, 2013.

KAUR, K.; MOHAN, N.; SANDHU, P. S. Reusability of Software Components using J48 Decision Tree. **International Conference on Artificial Intelligence and Embedded Systems (ICAIES'2012)**, p. 15-17, 2012.

KUMAR, V.; CHADHA, A. Mining Association Rules in Students' Assessment Data.

International Journal of Computer Science, v. 9, n. 5, p. 211-216, 2012.

LEE, I.; YONG, H.; ENGINEERING, C. S. Common Sense Knowledge Discovery for Association Rule. **IST**, v. 23, p. 188-191, 2013.

LIMA, D. DE. The military dictatorship, redemocratization and representative democracy in Brazil. **Revista Juridica - CCJ**, v. 16, n. 31, p. 75-92, 2012.

LUIZ, O. *étal.* Application of machine learning algorithms for data mining on beneficiaries of supplementary health plans. **Journal of Health Informatics**, v. 4, n. 2, p. 43-49, 2012.

NASSIF, D. R. J. **A tool for mining data from free software projects and creating socio-technical networks**. [s.l.] Universidade Tecnològica Federal do Paranâ, 2013.

OLIVEIRA, A. O estado da arte dos determinantes do voto no Brasil e as lacunas existentes. **Sociedade e Cultura**, v. 15, n. 1, p. 193-206, 17 oct. 2012.

OLIVEIRA, I. C. DE. **Application of Data Mining in the Search for an Infant Mortality Prevention Model**. [s.l.] Federal University of Santa Maria, 2001.

PADHY, N.; MISHRA, P.; PANIGRAHI, R. The Survey ofData Mining Applications And Feature Scope. **International Journal of Computer Science, Engineering and Information Technology**, v. 2, n. 3, p. 43-58, 2012.

PATIL, T. R.; SHEREKAR, S. S. Performance Analysis ofNaive Bayes and J48 Classification Algorithm for Data Classification. **International Journal Of Computer Science And Applications**, v. 6, n.2,2013.

RAVICHANDRAN, S.; SRINIVASAN, V. B.; RAMASAMY, C. Comparative Study on Decision Tree Techniques for Mobile Call Detail Record. **Journal of Communication and Computer**, v. 9, p.

1331-1335, 2012.

RODRIGUES, M. What determines the number of candidates in an election? **Economia & Tecnologia**, v. 25, 2011.

ROVEDDER, J. **Validation of object-oriented classification in Ikonos II satellite images and elaboration of georeferenced environmental indicators in the municipality of torres, coastal plain of Rio Grande do Sul, Brazil.** [s.l.] UFRGS - Federal University of Rio Grande do Sul, 2007.

SCHWERZ, A. L. *et al.* Predicting Developer Participation in Free Software Project Discussions. 2013.

SHWETA, M.; GARG, K. Mining Efficient Association Rules Through Apriori Algorithm Using Attributes and Comparative Analysis of Various Association Rule Algorithms.

International Journal of Advanced Research in Computer Science and Software Engineering, v. 3, n. 6, p. 306-312, 2013.

SILVA, I. A. F. **Knowledge discovery in an environmental monitoring database for water quality assessment**. [s.l.] Federal University of Mato Grosso, 2007.

SUNDAR, N. A.; LATHA, P. P.; CHANDRA, M. R. PERFORMANCE ANALYSIS OF CLASSIFICATION DATA MINING TECHNIQUES OVER HEART DISEASE DATA BASE. **International Journal of Engineering Science & Advanced Technology**, v. 2,n.3, p. 470-478, 2012.

WITTEN, I. H.; FRANK, E. **Data Mining: Practical Machine Learning Tools and Techniques, Second Edition**. San Francisco, CA, USA: Morgan Kaufmann Publishers Inc., 2005.

More Books!

yes
I want morebooks!

Buy your books fast and straightforward online - at one of world's fastest growing online book stores! Environmentally sound due to Print-on-Demand technologies.

Buy your books online at
www.morebooks.shop

Kaufen Sie Ihre Bücher schnell und unkompliziert online – auf einer der am schnellsten wachsenden Buchhandelsplattformen weltweit! Dank Print-On-Demand umwelt- und ressourcenschonend produzi ert.

Bücher schneller online kaufen
www.morebooks.shop

info@omniscriptum.com
www.omniscriptum.com

OMNIScriptum